Phoenix

Raquel Costa

Presentation by *BookLeaf Publishing*

Web: www.bookleafpub.com

E-mail: info@bookleafpub.com

ISBN: 978-93-5744-484-2

First edition 2022

To all those who wake up in the morning sore, broken, and scarred, and still somehow find the strength to make it through the day

ACKNOWLEDGEMENT

I want to thank my family and my boyfriend Fernando above all for supporting me through all the changes and difficult moments of my life.
I also want to thank my friends, now spread across the world. Your kindness made it possible to not only survive but also to thrive and grow. Being alone in a new place can be terrifying at times but thanks to you, I have been able to make a home, many homes, all over the world.
To my students, who have touched my heart deeply and without whom I would definitely not be here. I remember you all every single day and know that you are in my heart and in my prayers, always.
Lastly, to BookLeaf Publishing for making this book a reality. I couldn't have done it without you all and I'm eternally grateful.

PREFACE

During the pandemic and these uncertain times, the demand placed on us to be resilient, to go out and fight another day and to adapt to constant change as if it's nothing can sometimes feel extremely overwhelming.

It can feel like we'll never stop being thrashed back and forth, and for me at least, it's made me work a lot harder to find moments of peace, of rest and recuperation so that at least, when I have to fight, I won't be hurt to the point of inaction.

Recently I have also made the radical change of moving to a new country alone which has been a challenging experience. Feeling like your roots are in a different place can leave you feeling severely misplaced. However, it also has the beautiful flip-side that is finding who you are outside of your natural context. Redefining yourself and learning what it takes to make your heart feel at home no matter how far you go can truly be an enriching experience.

This book is about how I fight with loneliness and negative thoughts daily by focusing on the things that make me feel connected to myself.

Breaking apart doesn't have to be all bad, sometimes it's extremely necessary. Sometimes it's a reminder that we need to prioritise rest and self-care in order to rise again, just like a phoenix and keep facing whatever challenges life throws our direction. It's important to take moments to put the world on pause and do our "wintering" so that we are then able to rise on a sunnier day and face everything with a different attitude.

Emerging

Emerging from the ashes like so much of a
phoenix
Rising up again like I should
Rising up because they tell me it's over
Far away, not you, not now
Like it never happened, a dream of the past,
Just that.

They tell me it's my duty to fight another day
but I know I must find
my own reasons
If I burn it will be my flame
If I bleed it will be my blood

I hardly felt the fire when I rose
covered in ashes, ready to start again

The train

My eyelids flutter shut on the train journey
I
feel like I've been travelling forever and
I know that
this journey is just one of thousands
Thousands of simple pointless journeys

I always wanted to have a magnificent quest
Not so much a journey but an adventure
I scoffed at all these pointless trips
They meant nothing against the hope of
magnificence
But now I see that all these little journeys ARE
the magnificence
Together they make up the biggest quest I'll ever be on
The quest to live, love, and experience life every moment

These days I wish one of these trips would last
just a little longer
To give me some semblance of a home I lost
but I know
My home was never a destination
My home was always on the train
So for all I'm worth
the best I can do is
open my eyes

To stay

What would I learn if I stayed
for a time in one place instead of
hopping around like a rabid rabbit who
doesn't even know what it's late for
Wouldn't it be nice to just be and live
in wonder of all the things that
unfold around me while I sleep

The queen of hearts I'd, if only I could
preserve the only heart that matters
Instead of getting lost in endless rounds of croquet
A game I'm bound to win but for what?

What do I win by proving I can when
 I could all along
What would it be like to stay
like a mole underground in the winter
cosy in the darkness and safety
of my homely abode
I wish, sometimes
that I could live just a little shallower
instead of digging all the time
It is here; the gold I am searching for
is the light of the morning sun

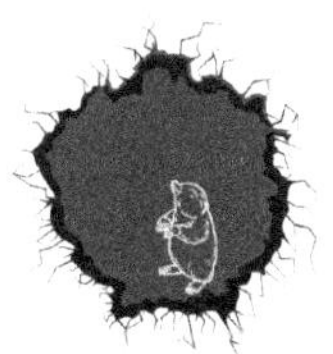

Not so easy

After the runway it's crazy to me how
something that had once seemed
Enormous and Unsurmountable
A lousy heavy trick of destiny is now just a collection
of plastic figurine trees
What I leave is not my home but it is my heart

Who would have thought
that it would be so easy
To get on a plane, to leave it all behind
and yet
so hard
To live divided between fairytale worlds
of plastic trees
It wasn't ever something permanent
There was always an invisible choice
And now that I make that choice
It's not so easy anymore

I never feared

I never feared the dark night
until the stars started to gossip about me
and the rain started coming down
I wasn't sure who I wanted to be but the night
never lied to me

Until every tree took the shape of the demons
inside my head
Until every path seemed to lead nowhere
or loop back without end in sight
Until the swings in the park just moved back and
forth without anyone swinging
and even the waters of the river gave
                no answers

I don't know what's ahead
and so I venture out alone
In the cold of the night
I sing songs to the river for direction
and I never quite know
what I'm hearing in the signs of the stars and the
river as it flows

All I know is that night in and night out I will
face the cold
for the hope that something great is coming

Because I fear, I fear, I fear
but hope is the last to die

Back to the future

I'm making projects for a time that won't come
fast enough
I wish I could race to the safety of a soft sofa
somewhere in the living room of my 40s or 50s
Because the high-speed roller coaster of my 20s
is sometimes too dizzying for even an adrenaline junkie
like myself

I know that so many people long for the
adventure I'm living,
dripped in privilege and possibility
More like drenched
It sounds so spoilt to give it up for a safe cottage
In the woods and a simple life

But the few times I saw what a gift a warm fire
can be
with a set of strong hands holding you close
I thought that maybe
A palace of gold is overrated
or the power to control it all

How useless it seems
compared to the beautiful, safe predictability of
a warm soup
his hands

and my favourite show
repeated again and again on the best episodes

Sometimes I would throw away the fertiliser and
just focus on my roots
by keeping my feet nice and warm
in comfy socks

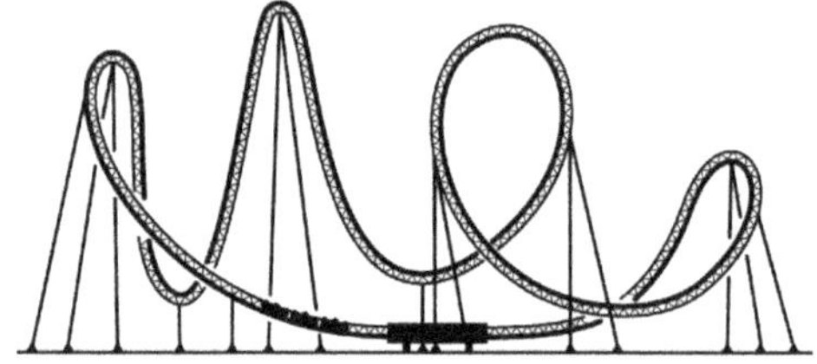

A simple life

To be here and spread my wings
is all I've ever loved and wanted
It's all I ever dreamed
and the glorious statues of my heroes
shine bright in the shadow of my
rainbow world

I see the possibility of my name in lights
and my sparkly jewelled shoes running down
hallways filled with gold
I see all this meaningless beauty from
the fact that I could leave it all behind
to find something worth fighting for

But what is a fight worth if the prize is not
peace?
In the end
the love, beauty, and kindness of a simple life
are all that's really worth fighting for

Wintering

These dark days I just wish I could burrow
under my blankets and never see the light of day
until spring
I just wish I could hibernate
like a bear in the winter
In my cave until better days arrived

Until the rays of sunshine sparkled
and all the snow of these days melted
I wouldn't go out until I could dance
careless and without fear
drinking through a straw, the possibilities to feel the rush
The thrills of summer are life-affirming
but the cosiness of winter
has stories to tell

Particularly about a girl who was always dancing
even when the world looked dark
The sun shone through the lamp in the bedroom
and the living room fire,
the warmth of family hugs was
a thousand times better than any summer sun

Open a window

They say that the trick to deal with grief
is to open the window just a little wider each day
until gradually, we can bear to see the light
It's funny how
even light can be
unbearable
when it doesn't match what we feel

I choose so many times to be in darkness
Sometimes it just matches my mood better
or sometimes I just forget that
there is more than these four walls

I've done incredible things
Breaking barriers and overcoming has become
an everyday
and yet it's crazy how
so many times I choose to sit in darkness
because I can't bear the light
My own light
can be too much

These days I'd rather
keep my eyes and blinds closed
and wait for the light to catch me
on a sunnier day

Best friend

I'm my own best friend
When I tuck my bed tighter
and choose colourful pillows and throws
When I make fresh cinnamon coffee
and dance to my favourite tunes
When the best show plays on repeat
and when a walk to the river takes priority
over anything I must do

That's when I find you,
My best friend
waiting in the trees like Huckleberry Finn
Into the cold lake barefoot
I don't care if I sneeze
I'll laugh louder

And scare the bad days away like a fever
I'll bring back summer with a smile
By letting it all hang out
and dance like it's Friday
Every day of the week
I'll breathe in the sunrise like Iced Tea
And never let a tear fall through my eyes
As long as the light lasts

The boat

Let's take a boat
to the middle of the lake that is your mind
I want to see the flowers and toads
I want to run my fingers through the water
and feel the flow of your thoughts
the lights that reflect on your surface,
and the roots that keep you grounded

Let me swim inside your brain for a while
until it gets dark and there's nowhere to go
My hair dripping, shivering wet
We sit together and count our dreams on stars
We snuggle up warm and away from the world
The boat left aside, we can walk back
We know the way now

To pray

I release another prayer
Each day I pray slower but better
I see things a little more clearly
I know that the world is not black and white
but grey
and gradually I find
I'm more able to accept
the little inconsistencies in life

I eat wholesome and bright
I drink with glee and dance with conviction
I write with love, speak with power and sing for joy
It matters only
when it's done for a reason
To see beauty with the eyes of a child at play
and to pray my dear, to pray

Art

Sometimes I forget even my favourite songs
On my worst days
I can't see how the lines on my painting
reflect every scar on my body and mind
but they don't bleed pain

Despite what you might think, they breed life
they see lightness in my future
even when I can't
they see colour in my life
when I see black and white

My art speaks volumes about me
Than I'll ever be able to express
(Or impress)
and when I dance
the world spins around in flashes
and the chaos of life makes sense
The chaos of living looks worth it
So I take another breath
and I dance another day

Nature

I don't want to think about anything
but my clicking, tapping pen
I don't want to dance with anyone
but the wind and the sun
Filling my cup with hope

I don't want to talk to anyone else but the river
These days no sound is finer than the birds and
the rustling of trees
No smell more perfect
than the earth beneath my feet
I want to embrace only the sunset
and laugh only with the dawn of the sun,
rising through my window
I only want to smoke fresh air,
the gift of nature and life

I am dust, I know it well
It's not daunting to know I belong to the earth
Liberating to find
I don't have to be anything more

Than earth, than water, than air, than fire,
than me

Blank pages

I love blank pages for they are
full of possibilities
full of room to expand and learn and break all the rules
without anyone telling you to
shut up or sit down or sit still or stop fidgeting

A blank page is the place to fidget with reality
so that it can start to make more sense
to organize chaos into clear lines of writing
Explosive but controlled
like my head, after I settle
My poems run over the place
that they should
They expand until they grow bigger than me
so I can see life from a distance, clearer than crystal,
clearer than ever before

Change perspective

I'll change bench and change perspective
a thousand times if needed
however long it takes
to not hurt my future with my path
I don't like to make plans
but I make plans for you

Until I fall sideways and can't breathe anymore
you'll be my reason to stand another day
and I'll change perspective a thousand times
until the only path in my future
is the path that leads to you
to your arms around me
and earth and water embracing us as their own

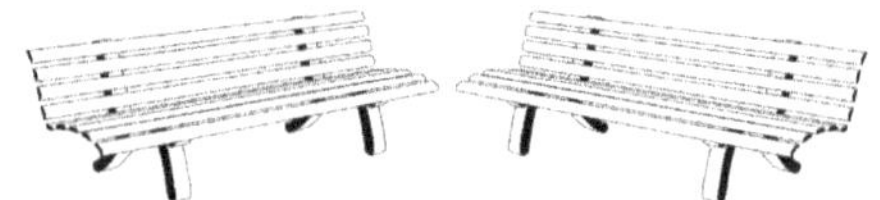

Who's that girl

Who's that girl
who dances with her eyes closed as if there's
only right now
and tomorrow will never come
It never wants to
Time just stops when she moves her hips

She sees the steps to Heaven
It doesn't seem so far after all

She doesn't see or hear the world
Just the enchanter's snake of a beat
that keeps her swaying like she'll never stop
Forgets what's behind
and the past
A horrid screech of hurt and pain
       dissolves
It means nothing when she sees
herself through the eyes
that don't see her but see movement
Her rhythm and vibration flow out of her veins
like fountains
She doesn't care about being seen with desire

Who cares, it's not
At all the same as knowing the dusty

briefcase she hides under her bed
Who wants to see that?
It's better to see her hips swaying,
arms waving in the moonlight
She doesn't care because time stops

She'll dream in colour but see in black and white
Who cares?
In a moment where it doesn't matter
Who cares?
She's alive

Firework

Flash, bang
I feel
like fireworks on bonfire night
When they fly through the sky just to die
Like me, I fly just to die everyday
and sometimes I don't quite know
what the point of the whole thing is
I just die again and again, just to burst into
colours

At the most unexpected moment
I will rise and find that I can bend into almost any shape
of myself that I desire
except fit into a crooked old box
at the bottom of the stairs
unseen and unused
gathering dust, moths and spiders
I'll rise tomorrow with a plan to break free
if it's not too late

I found my voice this time

I found my voice this time
I'll run like a tiger
and roar like a lioness until the ground
shakes and crumbles under my feet
It makes no sense for the world to be whole
when I myself am breaking apart
into tiny indistinguishable pieces that I am
still learning to put back together

I'm like a jigsaw puzzle that got all mixed up
with several pieces from different landscapes
and colours that just don't go together
I thought one day that I belonged and life was
simple
but what an illusion it was

Now I've learned
to scream again
like I haven't since I was born
I now know to make myself heard
over the sound of a thousand demons that posed
as friends

All my life, they have followed me and I thought
I even started to look a little like them
But I'm a lioness and always was

The fire's always been burning
keeping my core warm and lighting
my eyes with anxious flame
Now it's time
to light it up and let them see how it was
here all along

I see now

I see now
the sense in being the way I am
the loving way I love, I know
I move in my own way
in all ways
and ultimately,
though it looks different from all the
paths I've seen before,
from all the paths of other people
it works for me and it makes sense
I see and know right now
that it will take me where I need to go

Goodbye

A goodbye is good
when it means leaving behind all the rotten
damage
that filled the corners of my brain
like the trash I forgot to take out two weeks in a row

And goodbye is good when it burns away the
dirt and the pain of the past
to make space for regrowth and renewal
I rise even in winter
I know I'll keep fighting even when it seems
there is nothing
left to give or to gain

I'm here to defend the endless possibility that is life
Mine and yours
What we create, together
has the power to light up night skies and party rooms
I will fight for you with the gentleness
needed for those freezing nights
I'll wrap you in my blankets and make you tea
We're warriors at rest
and together we'll wait for the sun to come out
again